100
TRANSFORMATIVE
THOUGHTS
FOR WORK
& CAREER

100 TRANSFORMATIVE THOUGHTS FOR WORK & CAREER

aaron pang

Author of Unstuck

Also by Aaron Pang

Transformative Thoughts Series:
Transformative Thoughts for Intentional Living
Transformative Thoughts for Dads
Transformative Thoughts for Relationships and Love
Transformative Thoughts for Work & Career
Unstuck - Think Like A Kid And Free Your Mind
Reborn Digital
The Asian Dad

Contents

I won't find it
Stopping tell me
I can add value in someone else's life
Because at the end of the day
Other candidates are better
I don't have the experience
The economy is bad
And don't try to tell me that
Every rejection I get takes me one step
closer to where I want to be
Because deep down I know
I should just give up
And nothing you say will make me believe
I will find that YES in this world

(Now read bottom up)

We can. We can't. It's all in our head.

DAY 1

Navigating Work Realities

It's better to work for a good
manager in a bad company than a
bad manager in a good company.

DAY 2

Embracing Personal Leadership

whether you are an individual
contributor or manager, there is always
one person you can lead. You.

DAY 3

The Impact of Culture

You can try to change the
culture. But don't forget the
culture can change you too.

14

DAY 4

Shedding the
Mask at Work

It's exhausting trying to be someone
you are not. Are you done covering?

Empowering Yourself and Taking Control in the Workplace

You don't have control over who you meet at work. You have control over how you want to make an impact.

DAY 6

Surrounding Yourself
with Believers

It's easier to surround yourself with
people who believe in you instead of
trying to convince those who doubt you.

Golden Rule of Communication

Talk to others as you want to
be spoken to. Treat others as
you want to be treated.

DAY 8

Your Own Reflection

The only competition you have is the
person standing in front of the mirror.

DAY 9

Beyond the Title

Being a manager or a leader is much
more than the title. It's about taking care
of the people you are responsible for.

DAY 10

Technological and
Human Synergy

Technology will only replace you if you
don't seek to understand technology.

Unlocking Resourcefulness

If you want to be resourceful at
work, aim to become a comb-shaped,
t-shaped or pi-shaped talent.

Embracing Diverse Possibilities

Sample different career paths,
never commit to something
or specialise too early.

The Key to Progress
at Work

Knowing when to persevere and when
to pivot can help you break free.

Rejection and Acceptance

Every rejection you get takes you
one step closer to acceptance.

Distinguishing Your Worth at Work

Your job title is not your identity.
Don't confuse the two.

DAY 16

Appreciating Every Connection

Be grateful for everyone who has
come into your life at work.

A Priceless Gift for Personal Growth

Feedback is a gift. Treat it as learning cue and thank the person who is investing their time to help you grow.

Prioritizing Your
Greatest Asset

No job is worth your health. Prioritise
your health and mind first.

DAY 19

Breaking the Myth

The cult of "head start" is not true.

Embracing Diverse Career Choices

Most people end up choosing a different field than what they studied.

DAY 21

Purposeful Entrepreneurship

The best job in the world is to
work for yourself while solving
the world's problems.

Taking Charge of Your Destiny

Set goals and schedules for yourself, or you will forever be working towards someone else's goals and schedules.

Work-Life Balance

work is a subset of your life. It
supports your purpose. It should
never consume your life.

The Health-
Wealth Paradox

when we are young, we use our health
to buy wealth. when we get older,
we use our wealth to buy health.

DAY 25

A Universal Need

Self care is one-size-fits-
all. Everyone needs it.

Valuing Every Interaction and Contribution

Give everyone the best of you,
not the remainder of you.

The Freedom to Choose
Your Career Journey

Not everyone needs to be a leader.
Not everyone needs to climb up
the ladder. Some people are just
comfortable with where they are.

DAY 28

Mastering Management

Most of us know how to be an
individual contributor. Few of us
know how to be a manager.

DAY 29

When It's Time for a Career Change

If you feel dread going to work,
it's time to rethink how long you
want to keep doing it for.

Seizing the
Opportunities Today

The best time to build a personal
brand was yesterday. The
second best time is now.

Knowledge Monetization

we all know something or possess
knowledge that someone doesn't
know about. Find the audience who
can benefit from your knowledge.
Monetise the knowledge arbitrage.

Protecting Your Team for Optimal Performance

Being a leader is about being that shield where you can protect your people from unnecessary stresses and distractions so that they can be at their best.

The Power of Deep Work

Give yourself permission to do deep
work, not lots of shallow work.

Balancing Accessibility and Focus

You don't need to be accessible to everyone all the time. Set healthy boundaries and train your boss and your peers so you are not expected to be switched on all the time.

Productivity vs. Busyness

There is a big difference between
being busy and being productive.
Filling up your schedule with lots of
replicable tasks makes you busy,
but not necessarily productive.

Continuous Growth

The best career development advice
is to keep growing through learning and
trying things that you don't know.

A Culture of Learning and Trying

A good company rewards its people for trying, and doesn't reprimand its people for failing.

Seizing Opportunities Beyond One Source

You are always one conversation, one person away from your dream job. Never base your decision on a single person, a single source of data.

DAY 39

Redundancy with Dignity

Being made redundant is not
something to feel shameful about.

Humanity Begets Humanity

If you want to engage and recruit the best talents in the industry, start treating your people like humans. They are not resources. They are not a number on a spreadsheet. They are not an employee ID number.

Overcoming the Ego

Your ego is stopping you
from progressing.

Becoming the
Leader You Seek

Be the leader you wish you had. Be
the manager you wish you had.

DAY 43

Persistence in Pursuit

If you haven't found it yet, keep looking.

DAY 44

Possibility and Limitation

It's impossible. It's possible.
They're both right.

Employability and Versatility

If you want to improve your employability, build your transferrable skill.

Diversifying to Thrive

You can be loyal to your company but
you don't need to be loyal to your
industry. Build strengths in multiple
industries to prevent cyclical recession.

Preparing for the Future of Work

Technology will replace jobs. If you don't want to be replaced, do these two things. Understand where technology is going and how it will make your job obsolete. Invest in new skills that are hard for machines to replicate.

Choosing Your Response
to Challenges

You can choose to be bitter,
or choose to be better.

DAY 49

The Right Mix

Hard work alone doesn't guarantee
progress. But lacking hard
work guarantees failure.

Differentiating Hope
from Defeat

"You haven't found it yet" is not
the same as "you won't find it".

Unleashing Your
Full Potential

when you have a contingency
plan for everything, it stops
you from giving your best.

Choosing the Path of Giving

You are bound to meet takers and givers at work. And you have the freedom to make a conscious choice of which path you want to follow.

DAY 53

Earning Your Place

Nobody owes you anything at
work. You have to earn it.

The Golden Rule at Work

Treat people as you want to be
treated. Your people will treat your
customers as they want to be treated.

Balancing Values
and Decisions

Customers are not always right.
Employees are not always right.
Sometimes you need to make tough
decisions when values are not aligned.

From Complaints to Solutions

Complaining doesn't solve anything.
What is the issue here? How
can we solve it together?

Taking Charge of Your
Work Happiness

If you are not happy about something at work, either do something about it, or quit.

Turning Weakness into Power

Your vulnerability can be a
source of strength.

Unleashing Your
Multifaceted Self

Your best self can vary at work.
You are a human, not a feature.

DAY 60

Opportunities
Beyond Obstacles

When one door closes, many doors
are waiting for you to unlock.

Multiple Streams
of Revenue

Never rely on a single income from
one job. Always be on the lookout
for multiple income streams.
That's how you diversity risks.

Surrounding Yourself with Different Perspectives

Surround yourself with people who are
different to you, who challenge you.

73

Passion at Work

When you don't have passion for
what you do, it feels like work and
it grinds you down. When you have
passion for the work that you do, you
feel fulfilled and it motivates you.

Prioritising Family, Health, and Relationships

work can wait. Your family, your
health, your relationship can't wait.

Effective Communication

Messenger is a waste of time. If
things are urgent, they will call you.

Creating an Optimal Work Environment

If you want to practise mastery at work, first, switch off all your notifications. Second, set your messenger to "do not disturb". Third, close all the non-essential applications in the background. Find yourself a quiet room and disconnect from the world.

DAY 67

Finding Balance

Your work is not your private
life. Don't confuse the two.

78

Health and Wellbeing at Work

Sedentary behaviours and prolonged periods of working at your desk are sure-fire ways to add to your long-term medical bill. Set up reminders and take regular breaks. Drink lots of water. Go for a walk.

DAY 69

Diminishing Returns

Working long hours doesn't make you
more efficient. It only shows that
you are incapable of managing time
and expectations effectively.

Tech Neck

Neck muscles, tendons and ligaments support about ten to twelve pounds of your head. Looking down at your laptop or smartphone, with your chin to your chest, you are putting about 60 pounds of force on your neck.

DAY 71

Career Growth and Authenticity

Authenticity is a choice. If you want
to have better career prospects,
start making better choices.

Learning to Say No

Never feel pressured to say yes to every opportunity that comes your way. For every yes you say, you are also saying no to other things.

Finding Your Dream Job that Aligns with Your Purpose

Your dream job should support your
purpose in life. It should excite
you about why you are here.

Character in Action

Always talk to your peers as you want to be spoken to. A person's character shows when no one is watching them.

DAY 75

Lasting Interactions

Speak to and treat everyone at work like
it's your last time interacting with them.

Kindness and Compassion at Work

Everyone is dealing with something in life. How much do you know about your colleagues? Kindness is free.

Taking Action for Positive Change

Optimism is just as toxic as pessimism. Whining about your workplace is just as bad as hoping things will magically improve tomorrow. If there's something you are not happy about, do something about it. Be the change motion.

Value in the Workplace

Be obsessed with self development
and become so indispensable that
work can never replace you. Not
everyone is replaceable. Those who can
demonstrate value and adapt to change
also have a place in the job market.

DAY 79

Incremental Steps

The path to your career goal is seldom linear. Sometimes you might need to take two steps backward in order to leap one step forward. Setback is progress made.

Learning Journey

Feeling lost? Stuck? These are learning cues for your self-development, and you are just early in the process.

Balancing Capability and Ego

Your untapped potential is the
difference between what you
are capable of and your ego.

The Power of Emotional Intelligence

Technical skills can only get you
so far. You need emotional skills
and social integration underneath
the iceberg to steer the ship.

Developing Non-Negotiable Systems

Motivation comes and goes. Develop
a non-negotiable system and ritual to
help you produce consistent results.
Successful people are trained, not born.

DAY 84

The Cult of Head Start

Distractions are omnipresent. The
promotion you missed. The payrise
that feels overdue. Stay in your lane.
If you are not appreciated in your
environment, change the environment.

The Currency of
Positive Relationships

Respect is a free currency.

The Growth of Others

Be interested instead of
interesting. People care about
how you can help them grow.

DAY 87

Abundance in Generosity

The more you give, the more you will
receive. Don't mind the takers, just play
your game. Stay true to yourself.

Indistractibility in Focus

Be so focused on your work that
you are indestructible no matter
the environment you are in.

Block Your Calendar

Block your lunch hour. Set up time
blocks for focused work. Protect your
sanctuary and your path to mastery.

The 80/20 Rule

80% of your impact comes from 20% of your effort. How can you get rid of the 80% effort that yields less or no impact?

DAY 91

Time for Multitask Detox

Studies show that 98% of us
are monotaskers and only 2%
are supertaskers. Are you
addicted to multi-tasking?

Management by Absence

Turn off your phone when you
are on leave. If you need to be
contacted while you are away, there's
either something wrong with the
company or something wrong with
how you are managing your time.

Fostering Inclusivity and Participation

Design your meeting with intention. An inclusive meeting is more than just asking everyone to speak up. It provides opportunities for different people to express their thoughts and feelings before, during and after the meeting via different cues such as polls, emails and conversations. Simply asking others to contribute during a meeting assumes everyone is comfortable to speak up spontaneously. The quiet ones often have great ideas.

Encouraging Equal Participation

An inclusive workplace is one that encourages equal participation from everyone irrespective of their background.

DAY 95

Authentic Conversations

One-on-one is not a quarterly or half-yearly formality, it is a daily responsibility. Show interest in people's lives and they will show interest in yours.

Transformational Offboarding

When someone leaves an organisation, it is the start of a new relationship. Be grateful for their work. Wish them well.

Walk the Talk in Interviews

How did you lead yourself this year?
How many people have you helped? what
lives have you impacted? what tough
decisions did you make by adhering
to your values? what drives you?

Takers at the Table

Takers eat your culture for breakfast.

The "CEO" Position

Don't expect everyone to be like
you or to have the same motivations
as you. Some people are happy
with where they are. They have
children to look after. They have
their health to look after. They've
already found their "CEO" position.

The 100% Fallacy

In a workplace, there are single working
parents who can't afford to miss a
single day of work, who can't be sick
because no one will look after their
children. Their self-care comes last
on the pecking order. And then there
are people who are dealing with family,
health and finance issues. Be realistic
with your expectations of others. No
one can ever be 100% all the time.

More Resources

Thank you for reading this book from beginning to end. I really appreciate your time and presence throughout. I would love to hear from you. Please take a picture and share your favourites with me and those who need more dopamine!

If you would like to receive updates on the latest content, you can also follow these platforms below:

Newsletter: Receive transformative ideas at
www.TransformativePurpose.com

Podcast: Search 'Transformative Purpose'
on your favourite podcast player.

YouTube: @TransformativePurpose

Linkedin: @AaronPang

Instagram: @AaronTPang

Medium: @AaronTPang

Facebook: @TransformativePurpose

Better together!

About Aaron Pang

"Feeling stuck is our invitation to grow in life. People who have a clear purpose can also be unhappy. We don't rise to the level of our purpose—we fall to the level of our transformative mindset, system and consistent actions."

A major life event on the night of April 7th, 2019, changed Aaron Pang's life narrative forever and inspired him to look inward. Feeling guilty and seeing himself as an incompetent father, he realised he simply didn't know what his PURPOSE in life was.

At the age of 35, Aaron had no book and no writing or podcasting experience. Unexpectedly, his negative emotions became his greatest motivator. His story is living proof that you're never too late to start something you love.

Founder of Transformative Purpose and Industry Advisor to Microsoft, Aaron Pang's popular book Unstuck—Think Like a Kid and Free Your Mind is a bestseller on Amazon and in Hong Kong. He is a sought-after motivational and transformational speaker, and hosts a top 3% globally ranked self-development podcast.

Aaron was recognised by the Australia China Alumni Association as the winner of the Australia China Alumni Award in 2022. His honest insights on success, motivation and mindset—as well as his vulnerable sharing and ability to develop authentic conversations—have made him a thought leader in personal growth.

Aaron works with corporates and schools to help leaders, professionals, parents and young people develop a transformative mindset through his unique "kid height" approach. His experience in business has given him a rare breadth of general management and leadership opportunities spanning across business transformation, management consulting and entrepreneurship.

Aaron lives in Hong Kong with his wife and two young boys.